Wonder around the World

experience™
Early Learning

First published by Experience Early Learning Company
7243 Scotchwood Lane, Grawn, Michigan 49637 USA

ISBN 978-1-937954-12-3
Visit us at **www.ExperienceEarlyLearning.com**

By plane, train, car and boat,
come with us on a trip to
wonders all over the world.

Along the way, we'll wonder about
all the wonderful things we can do!

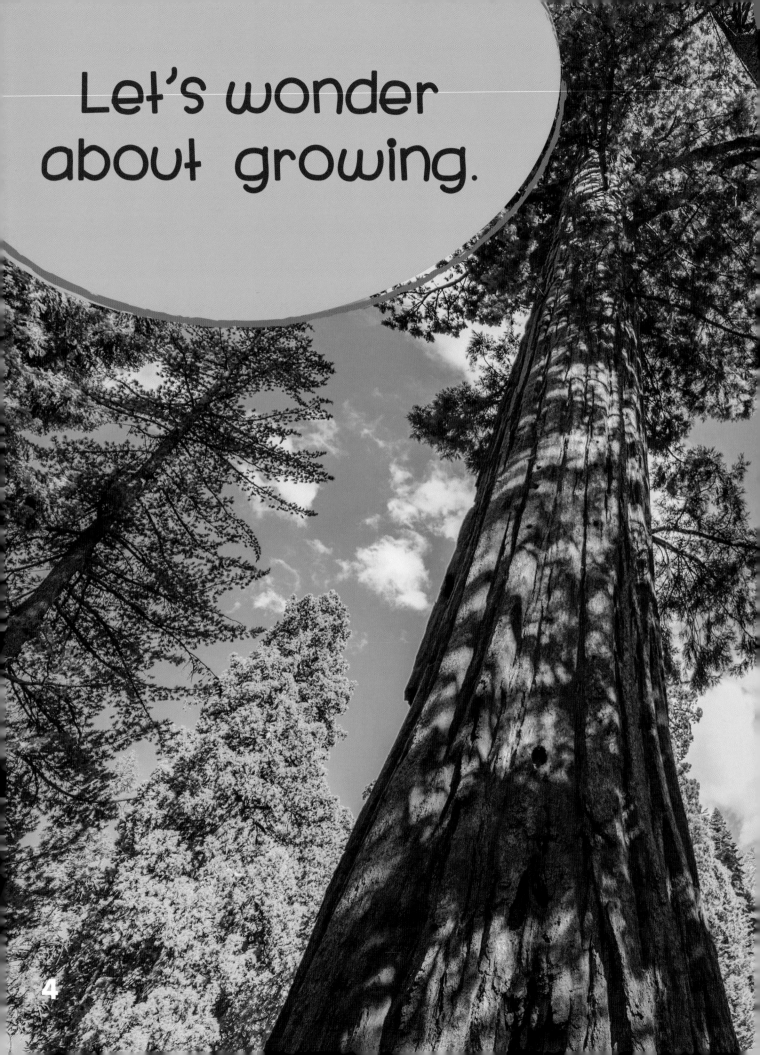

Let's wonder about growing.

4

What can you see growing tall and wide near you?

5

Giant Sequoia Trees

Giant Sequoias are the largest trees in the world.

They are very tall and very wide.

Giant Sequoias grow near the west coast of the United States.

Each year a tree adds another ring.

How many rings can you touch?

Some sequoias are so wide that you can drive through them!

Let's go and wonder more!

Let's wonder about stacking.

What kinds of layers can you stack?

The Grand Canyon

The Grand Canyon has many layers of stacked rock.

The Colorado River cut through the rock layers and formed the canyon.

The Grand Canyon is in North America, in the southwest U.S.

The Native American name for the canyon is "Kaibab." This means "mountain upside down."

Mules carry people and supplies down into the canyon.

Let's go and wonder more!

What do you think is stacked on the mules?

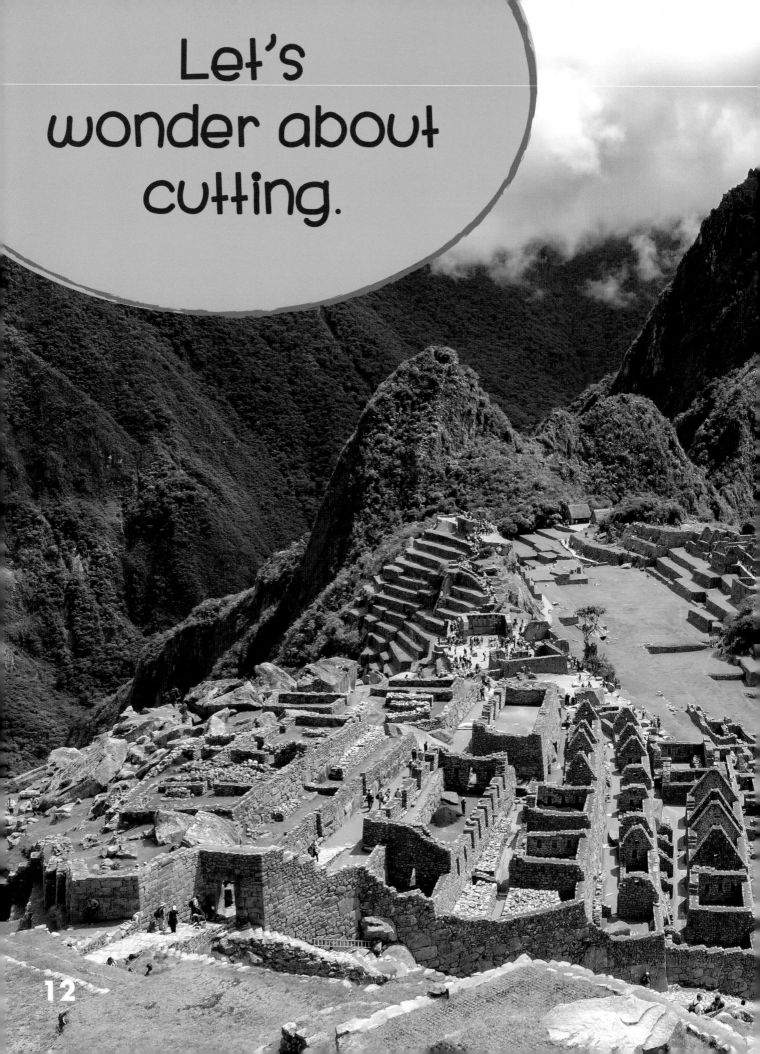

Let's wonder about cutting.

What types of materials can you cut?

13

Machu Picchu

Machu Picchu is an ancient city.

The builders cut into the side of the mountain and built a city with many stairs, windows and doors.

Machu Picchu is in South America, in the country of Peru.

The Incas cut stones to fit together like a puzzle.

What do you think the Incas used to cut these rocks?

Let's go and wonder more!

Where do you think this llama is going?

15

Let's wonder
about pouring.

16

How can you pour water at different speeds?

Victoria Falls

The mighty Zambezi River flows over Victoria Falls.

Almost 625 million liters of water pour over the edge per minute. That is a lot of water!

Victoria Falls is in the southern part of the African continent.

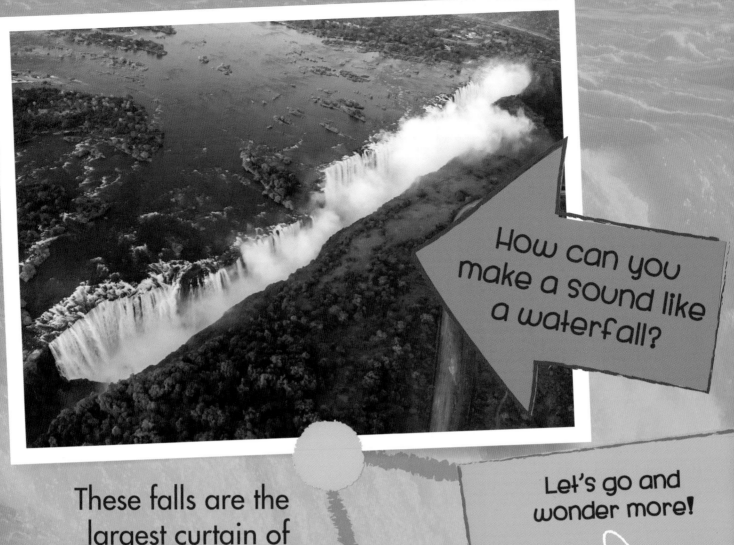

How can you make a sound like a waterfall?

These falls are the largest curtain of water in the world.

Let's go and wonder more!

Zebra, antelope, white rhinos and giraffe all live near the falls.

Let's wonder about building.

What can you
build with blocks?

21

The Great Pyramid

The Great Pyramid of Giza was the tallest building for thousands of years.

It took 20 years to build the pyramid. The builders pushed the blocks up a ramp and moved them into position with a lever.

The Great Pyramid is in Egypt on the African continent.

The Egyptians used a picture language to tell stories.

What do you think is happening in this story?

Let's go and wonder more!

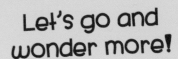

It took millions of blocks to build the pyramid.

The Leaning Tower of Pisa

The tower leans because the soil is softer on one side.

As a result, the tower sunk into the ground on that side.

The Leaning Tower of Pisa is in Europe, in the country of Italy.

What do you think would happen if this tower fell over?

Let's go and wonder more!

To clean and secure the tower, people put up scaffolding. It took twenty years to fix the tower.

27

Let's wonder about painting.

What colors
would you
want to paint
your home?

29

St. Basil's Cathedral

Ivan the Terrible had the cathedral built in 1552.

The cathedral has 9 onion domes. At first they were painted muted colors. But since the 1800s, painters discovered how to make brighter pigments. Now the cathedral looks like a rainbow of colors.

St. Basil's Cathedral is in Russia.

The cathedral was built to look like a bonfire rising into the sky.

How are these pictures similar?

Let's go and wonder more!

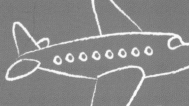

It is colorful on the inside, too!

Let's wonder
about climbing.

32

What can you climb?

Mt. Everest

Mt. Everest is very dangerous to climb. It is icy, steep and has cold, dangerous weather.

A special guide, called a Sherpa, takes climbers up the mountain. The climb can take up to 6 weeks.

Mt. Everest sits on the border between Nepal and China in Asia.

Many people try to climb Mt. Everest every year.

They camp at the base and wait for good weather.

Let's go and wonder more!

What looks dangerous on this mountain?

Climbers need oxygen tanks because the air is so thin near the peak.

35

Let's wonder
about
measuring.

What can you use to measure?

The Great Wall

The Great Wall of China is the longest wall in the world. It is over 5500 miles long.

It is difficult to measure because it goes over and around many mountains.

The Great Wall is in Asia and runs across China.

Some steps on the wall can be very steep. We use our hands and feet to climb them.

What do you think is at the top of these steep stairs?

We can count our steps to measure the distance between clay soldiers.

Let's go and wonder more!

Let's wonder about counting.

How many living
things can you
see and count?

41

The Great Barrier Reef

The Great Barrier Reef is the world's largest living structure.

Coral looks like a plant, but it is actually an animal. When you look at coral, you are seeing thousands of tiny animals called polyps.

The Great Barrier Reef is located in the Pacific Ocean off the coast of Australia.

The Great Barrier Reef is the only living thing on Earth you can see from space.

Let's go and wonder more!

How many fish can you count?

More than 1500 different kinds of fish live on the reef.

Let's wonder about forming.

What can you form out of clay or sand?

45

Ayers Rock

Ayers Rock is a large sandstone formation that used to be on the bottom of the sea. Now the rock is surrounded by a desert.

Ayers Rock is in the middle of Australia.

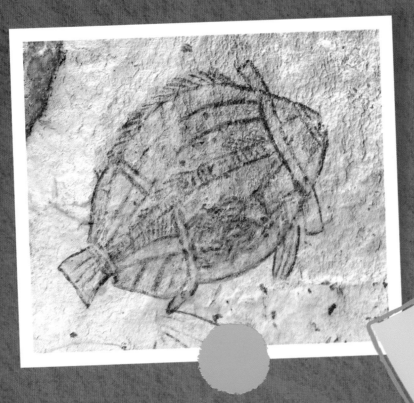

There are many caves in Ayers Rock.

The Aboriginals called the rock 'Uluru' and drew pictures inside the caves.

What would you draw on a rock?

Now let's head back home!

Be careful not to disturb the kangaroo.

Wonder around the world with me.
Grow, stack, cut, pour, build,

We started here...

The Grand Canyon

The Leaning Tower of Pisa

Giant Sequoias

Machu Picchu

lean, paint, climb, measure, count
and form new curiosities!

St. Basil's Cathedral

The Great Wall

The Great Pyramid

Mt. Everest

The Great Barrier Reef

Ayers Rock

Victoria Falls

We finished here!

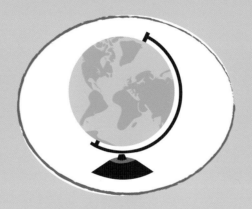